Harriette~
To my
"friend"
and
so much
more
fondly

THE BOOK OF
FRIENDSHIP

THE BOOK OF
FRIENDSHIP

EDITED BY MARY G. RODARTE

DESIGNED BY DIANE HOBBING

ARIEL BOOKS

**Andrews McMeel
Publishing**
Kansas City

ISBN: 0-7407-1945-9

Library of Congress Catalog Card Number: 2001086520

CONTENTS

INTRODUCTION   13

THE JOY OF FRIENDSHIP   17

The "Ten Commandments" of Friendship   18

Emma, by Jane Austen   25

"The Law of Friendship," by Jalal ad-Din ar-Rumi   27

"We talked as Girls do-," by Emily Dickinson   31

Olive, by Dinah Maria Mulock Craik   34

Fun Things for Friends to Do Together   40

"The Travelers and the Bear," by Aesop   44

Famous Friends: Patsy Cline and Louise Seger   50

Middlemarch, by George Eliot   53

"How Fast You Are!" Anonymous Chinese verse   60

Othello, by William Shakespeare   69

THE ART OF LETTER WRITING   77

Letter to Peter Abelard, from Héloïse   86

Letter to Lady Mary Fox Strangways, from Agnes Porter   89

Letter from Charlotte Brontë   96

Letter to Fanny Knight, from Jane Austen   98

Little Women, by Louisa May Alcott   104

"A Mile with Me," by Henry van Dyke   108

More Fun Things for Friends to Do Together   112

The Woman's Rose, by Olive Schreiner — 114

Letter to Charles Bray, from George Eliot — 126

Letter from Emily Dickinson — 128

Olive, by Dinah Maria Mulock Craik — 135

Famous Friends: Susan B. Anthony and Elizabeth Cady Stanton — 141

"Androcles and the Lion," by Aesop — 142

From the Journal of Agnes Porter — 151

Letter to Her Sister, Cassandra, from Jane Austen — 158

FOOD, FRIENDS, AND FUN   165

Old-fashioned Blueberry Muffins   172

Baked Pears in Ginger Cream   174

South-of-the-Border "Lasagna"   184

"For My Friend P'ei Ti," by Wang Wei   187

Letter to Sir David Dalrymple, from James Boswell   196

Letter to John Keats, from Benjamin Robert Haydon   198

Famous Friends: Georgia O'Keeffe and Anita Pollitzer   205

French Bread Pizza   214

Summery Spinach Salad   218

THE SWEETNESS OF FRIENDS 221

Orange Sugar Cookies 224

Gingerbread Friends 226

Untitled verse, by Makeda, Queen of Sheba 235

"A Night with My Friend," by Li Po 237

The Adventures of Huckleberry Finn, by Mark Twain 238

Letter to Lady Georgiana, from Sydney Smith 240

Letter to Charles Bray, from George Eliot 243

From the Journal of Annie Cooper 248

From the Journal of Agnes Porter 251

"One Sister have I in the house~," by Emily Dickinson 256

Untitled verse, by Lal Ded 263

Mocha Float 266

"The Trees and the Axe," by Aesop   272

"A Sister," by Christina Georgina Rossetti   283

"The Shelter," by Jalal ad-Din ar-Rumi   285

Even More Fun Things for Friends to Do Together   290

Letter to Sara Hennell, from George Eliot   297

Letter to Abiah Root, from Emily Dickinson   300

"Friendship," by Dinah Maria Mulock Craik   308

"We Have Been Friends Together," by Caroline Norton   311

Caribbean Delight   320

From the Journal of Agnes Porter   329

Letter to Sara Hennell, from George Eliot   330

Coffee Ecstasy   336

"All Paths Lead to You," by Blanche Shoemaker Wagstaff   338

"Friends Taking Their Leave," by Li Po   341

"Auld Lang Syne," by Robert Burns   347

Letter from Emily Dickinson   351

ost of us remember our first friend, whether it was the little girl with three pigtails who lived next door, or the boy who rode the bright blue bike to kindergarten class. Back then, friendship was easy; it was based on sharing a game of hopscotch, eating cake and ice cream at a birthday party, or playing for hours on a backyard swing set. Over time, some of those friendships grew into relationships that lasted throughout grade school, college, or even a lifetime, while others faded as quickly as they began.

Why do you choose one person over another to be your friend? Perhaps you share a common interest in sports or travel or painting. Or maybe you both dream of someday starting your own software business and you've been waiting for just the right partner to come along. Then again, friendship might have blossomed precisely because you were so different from one another. She loves adventure travel and you prefer to relax on a deserted beach. You admire her courage to explore new territory, and thoroughly enjoy her vivid accounts of foreign locales and unusual people.

Sometimes you meet someone who is an instant friend—the chemistry is just right—and you feel as if you've always known each other. You laugh at the same jokes and have uncannily similar philosophies about life and how to live it to the fullest.

On the other hand, some friendships may take years to develop. It's possible you met because your children were friends. You discovered mutual interests while gradually getting to know each other at the school bus stop or on weekends at the Little League game. But no matter how your friendship began or progressed, what's important is that you eventually found each other—kindred spirits to share the journey—to grow up together.

This book is filled with a collection of poems, letters (from the famous and not so famous), and excerpts from novels about the trials and tribulations of true friendship. There are delicious recipes to share and fun things to do together, eloquent insights about the significance of friendship, and interesting tidbits about famous pals. Possibly, they will inspire you to get in touch with an old friend or make a few new ones. But one thing's certain: The sentiments expressed are certain to make you cherish, even more, the good friends you're so lucky to already have.

THE JOY OF
FRIENDSHIP

The "Ten Commandments" of Friendship

I will not fail to keep in touch, whether by phone, letter, or e-mail.

I will boast and brag about my friend behind his or her back.

I will help my friend eat a pint of ice cream in times of celebration or commiseration.

I will not forget my friend's birthday.

I will not reveal my friend's true hair color or age to anyone, no matter how great the temptation.

I will return items I borrowed from my friend, including music, tools, and clothes.

I will not mention my friend's postholiday pounds.

I will guard my friend's secrets with my life.

I will not criticize my friend's driving skills, cooking expertise, or inability to tell a joke.

I will not ask anything of my friend that I would not ask of myself.

Friend

Where does the word *friend* come from? The Old English word *freo* meant "free"; "not in bondage"; "noble"; "glad." The Old English word *freon* means "to love," and the word *freoud* becomes the modern word *friend*.

From *Emma*
by Jane Austen

Miss Taylor married. It was Miss Taylor's loss which first brought grief. It was on the wedding-day of this beloved friend that Emma first sat in mournful thought of any continuance. . . . The want of Miss Taylor would be felt every hour of every day. . . . It had been a friend and companion such as few possessed, intelligent, well-informed, useful, gentle, knowing all the ways of the family, interested in all its concerns, and peculiarly interested in herself, in every pleasure, every scheme of hers;—one to whom she could speak every thought as it arose, and who had such an affection for her as could never find fault.

From "The Law of Friendship"
by Jalal ad-Din ar-Rumi

Those forces that draw friends together

do not obey the laws of nature. . . .

A hand moves our birdcages.

Some are brought closer, and some move apart.

Do not try to understand, but be aware

of who you are drawn to, and who you are not.

President Lincoln
Befriends a Soldier

Countless appeals for pardon came to President Lincoln from soldiers who faced military discipline. Each appeal was typically presented with accompanying letters from influential people who could vouch for the young man.

One day, a single sheet came before the president—an appeal from a soldier without any supporting documents.

"What!" exclaimed the President, "has this man no friends?"

"No, sir, not one," said the man presenting the appeal to him.

"Then," said Lincoln, "I will be his friend."

No. 9039

No. 9040

No 9041

No. 9042

No. 9044

No. 9045

No. 9046

No. 9047

From "We talked as Girls do—"

by Emily Dickinson

We talked as Girls do—

Fond, and late—

We speculated fair, on every subject, but the Grave—

Of our's, none affair—

We handled Destinies, as cool—

As we—Disposers—be—

And God, a Quiet Party

To our authority—

A Portrait of Friendship

Tomboy Idgie is as wild and independent as they come, but when quiet Ruth arrives to stay with Idgie's family for the summer, Idgie undergoes a remarkable transformation.

Everywhere Ruth was, that's where Idgie would be. It was a mutual thing. They just took to each  other, and you could hear them, sittin' on the swing on the porch, gigglin' all night.

—Fannie Flagg, *Fried Green Tomatoes at the Whistle Stop Cafe*

From *Olive*
by Dinah Maria Mulock Craik

. . . **B**ut none of these mysteries came to the knowledge of little Olive. She lived the dream-life of early girlhood—dwelling in an atmosphere still and pure as a grey spring morning, ere the sun has risen. All she learnt was from books; for though she had occasional teachers, she had never been sent to school.

Sometimes she regretted this, thinking how pleasant it would be to have companions, or at least one friend of her own age, to whom she might talk on the various subjects of which she had of late begun to dream. These never passed the still sanctuary of her own thoughts; for some instinct told her that her mother would scarce sympathise with her wild imaginations in Art and Poetry. So she thought of them always by herself, when she was strolling about the small but pleasant garden that sloped down from the back of the house to the river; or when, extending her peregrinations, she went to sit in the summer-house of the garden adjoining, which belonged to a large mansion close by, long uninhabited. It was quite a punishment to Olive when a family came to live there, and she lost the use of the beautiful, deserted garden.

Still, it was something new to have neighbours. She felt quite a curiosity respecting them, which was not diminished when, looking out one day from the stair-case window (a favourite seat, from which every night she watched the sun set), Olive caught a sight of the new occupants of her former haunts.

They were two little boys of about nine or ten, playing noisily enough—as boys will. Olive did not notice them much, except the youngest, who appeared much the quieter and gentler of the two; but her gaze rested a long time on a girl, who seemed to be their elder sister. She was walking by herself up and down an alley, with a shawl thrown over her head, and her thick, black hair blown about by the March winds. Olive thought she looked very picturesque . . .

For several days after, she took a deep interest in watching the family-party, and chiefly this young girl—partly because she was so pretty, and partly because she seemed nearly about her own age, or perhaps a year or two older. Olive often contrived to walk in her garden when her neighbours were in theirs—so that she could hear the boys' cheerful voices over the high hedge. By this means she learnt their Christian names, Robert, and Lyle—the latter of which she admired very much, and thought it exactly suited the pretty, delicate younger brother.

She wished much to find out that of their sister—but could not; for the elder girl took little notice of them, or they of her. So Olive, after thinking and talking of her for some time, as "my beauty next door," to Mrs. Rothesay's great amusement, at last christened her by the imaginary name of Maddalena.

After a few weeks, it seemed as though the interest between the young neighbours became mutual—for Olive, in her walks, sometimes fancied she saw faces watching her, too, from the staircase window. . . .

At last, when, one lovely spring evening, she stood leaning over the low wall at the garden's end, idly watching the river flow by beneath, she turned round, and saw fixed on her, with a curiosity not unmingled with interest, the dark eyes of "Maddalena." Somehow or other, the two girls smiled—and then the elder spoke.

"The evening was very fine,"

she said; "and it was rather dull, walking in the garden all alone."

Olive had never found it so; but she was used to it. Her young neighbour was not; she had always lived in a large town, &c. &c.

A few more simple nothings spun out the conversation for ten minutes. The next day it was resumed, and extended to twenty; during which Olive learnt that her young beauty's name, so far from being anything so fine as Maddalena, was plain Sarah—or Sara, as its owner took care to explain. Olive was rather disappointed—but she thought of Coleridge's ladye love; consoled herself, and tried to console the young lady, with repeating "My pensive Sara! thy soft cheek reclined," &c. At which Miss Sara Derwent laughed, and asked who wrote that very pretty poetry?

Olive was a little confounded. She fancied everybody read Coleridge, and her companion sank just one degree in her estimation. But as soon as she looked again on the charming face, with its large, languishing Asiatic eyes, and delicate mouth—just like that of the lotus-leaved "Clytie," which she loved so much,—Olive felt all her interest revive. Never was there any girl over whom every form of beauty exercised more fascination. By the week's end she was positively enchanted with her neighbour, and before a month had passed the two young girls had struck up that romantic friendship peculiar to sixteen.

Fun Things for Friends

- Take a walking tour (depending on where you live, it can be local or a weekend getaway) with one special friend or a group of friends to learn about a new place and more about each other. Some ideas: the city's botanical gardens, a historic neighborhood, or the local university campus.

- Spend several leisurely hours at your favorite coffee shop and split a piece of to-die-for layer cake.

to Do Together

- Have an old-fashioned slumber party. Rent favorite movies, pop popcorn, gossip, and behave as if you were sixteen again.

- Go to the zoo and talk to the animals.

- Buy an easy pattern (and quilted material) for funky beach or baby bags and spend the afternoon sewing.

A Portrait of Friendship

When Willa sinks all her money into a run-down house, people in town think she's made a big mistake. But Willa's good friends—the "Mamas"—come to her rescue.

We did one three-day stint of painting. . . . In the late afternoon, the Mamas jumped buck naked off the floating dock that extended into the river, and we swam and splashed one another. It was as if the pristine walls of Willa's new house belonged to us all.

—Colette Dowling, *Red Hot Mamas: Coming into Our Own at Fifty*

The Travelers and the Bear
by Aesop

One day two travelers came upon a bear. After the first had saved his skin by climbing a tree, the other, knowing he had no chance against the bear single-handed, threw himself on the ground and pretended to be dead. The bear came and sniffed around his ears but, thinking him to be dead, walked off. His friend asked, on descending from the tree, "What was the bear whispering in your ear?" "Oh, he just said I should think twice about travelling with people who run out on their friends."

Moral:
Misfortune tests
the sincerity of
friendship.

When you least expect it,
a common thread
—golden, at that—
begins to weave together
the fabric of friendship.

—Mary Kay Shanley

I find you in all small and lovely
things; in the little fishes like
flames in the green water, in the
furred and stupid softness of
bumble-bees fat as laughter,
in all the chiming radiance of
warmth and light and scent
in the summer garden.

—Winifred Holtby

Patsy Cline and Louise Seger

Louise Seger first heard Patsy Cline sing "Walkin' After Midnight" on *The Arthur Godfrey Show* in 1957. Like many others of the time, she fell in love with Patsy's voice. Louise was a big fan of Patsy's, and in 1961, attended a concert in Houston, where she met the singer in person. The two quickly struck up a friendship. Until the untimely, tragic airplane crash that took Patsy's life, the two friends often wrote to each other. Patsy signed her letters, "Always, Patsy Cline," and the phrase later became the title of a play that focuses on their unique friendship.

From *Middlemarch*
by George Eliot

Rosamond and Mary had been talking faster than their male friends. They did not think of sitting down, but stood at the toilette-table near the window . . .

"Oh, Mr. Lydgate!" said Mary, with an unmistakable lapse into indifference. "You want to know something about him," she added, not choosing to indulge Rosamond's indirectness.

"Merely, how you like him."

"There is no question of liking at present. My liking always wants some little kindness to kindle it. I am not magnanimous enough to like people who speak to me without seeming to see me."

"Is he so haughty?" said Rosamond, with heightened satisfaction. "You know that he is of good family?"

"No; he did not give that as a reason."

"Mary! You are the oddest girl. But what sort of looking man is he? Describe him to me."

"How can one describe a man? I can give you an inventory: heavy eyebrows, dark eyes, a straight nose, thick dark hair, large solid white hands—and—let me see—oh, an exquisite cambric pocket-handkerchief. But you will see him. You know this is about the time of his visits."

Rosamond blushed a little, but said, meditatively, "I rather like a haughty manner. I cannot endure a rattling young man."

"I did not tell you that Mr. Lydgate was haughty; but *il y en a pour tous les goûts,* as little Mamselle used to say, and if any girl can choose the particular sort of conceit she would like, I should think it is you, Rosy."

"Haughtiness is not conceit; I call Fred conceited."

"I wish no one said any worse of him. He should be more careful. Mrs. Waule has been telling uncle that Fred is very unsteady." Mary spoke from a girlish impulse which got the better of her judgment. There was a vague uneasiness associated with the word "unsteady" which she hoped Rosamond might say something to dissipate. But she purposely abstained from mentioning Mrs. Waule's more special insinuation.

"Oh, Fred is horrid!" said Rosamond. She would not have allowed herself so unsuitable a word to anyone but Mary.

"What do you mean by horrid?"

"He is so idle, and makes papa so angry, and says he will not take orders."

"I think Fred is quite right."

"How can you say he is quite right, Mary? I thought you had more sense of religion."

"He is not fit to be a clergy-man."

"But he ought to be fit."

"Well, then, he is not what he ought to be. I know some other people who are in the same case."

"But no one approves of them. I should not like to marry a clergyman; but there must be clergymen."

"It does not follow that Fred must be one."

"But when papa has been at the expense of educating him for it! And only suppose, if he should have no fortune left him?"

"I can suppose that very well," said Mary, dryly.

"Then I wonder you can defend Fred," said Rosamond, inclined to push this point.

"I don't defend him," said

Mary, laughing; "I would defend any parish from having him for a clergyman."

"But of course if he were a clergyman, he must be different."

"Yes, he would be a great hypocrite; and he is not that yet."

"It is of no use saying anything to you, Mary. You always take Fred's part."

"Why should I not take his part?" said Mary, lighting up. "He would take mine. He is the only person who takes the least trouble to oblige me."

"You make me feel very uncomfortable, Mary," said Rosamond, with her gravest mildness; "I would not tell mamma for the world."

"What would you not tell her?" said Mary, angrily.

"Pray do not go into a rage,

Mary," said Rosamond, mildly as ever.

"If your mamma is afraid that Fred will make me an offer, tell her that I would not marry him if he asked me. But he is not going to do so, that I am aware. He certainly never has asked me."

"Mary, you are always so violent."

"And you are always so exasperating."

"I? What can you blame me for?"

"Oh, blameless people are always the most exasperating. There is the bell—I think we must go down."

"I did not mean to quarrel," said Rosamond, putting on her hat.

"Quarrel? Nonsense; we have not quarrelled. If one is not to get into a rage sometimes, what is the good of being friends?"

"Am I to repeat what you have said?"

"Just as you please. I never say what I am afraid of having repeated. But let us go down."

How Fast You Are!

You met me at Mount Nao,

And together we chased after two boars.

You bowed to me, saying, "You are so agile!"

"Such a fine figure you are!"

You and I, on the road to Nao,

Together we chased two bucks.

You bowed to me, saying, "You are so handsome!"

"How skillful you are!"

You and I, on the sunny side of Nao,

Together we chased two wolves.

You bowed to me, saying, "You are the expert!"

—Anonymous Chinese verse

Pal

The word *pal* was borrowed from British Romany *pal,* meaning "brother" or "friend."

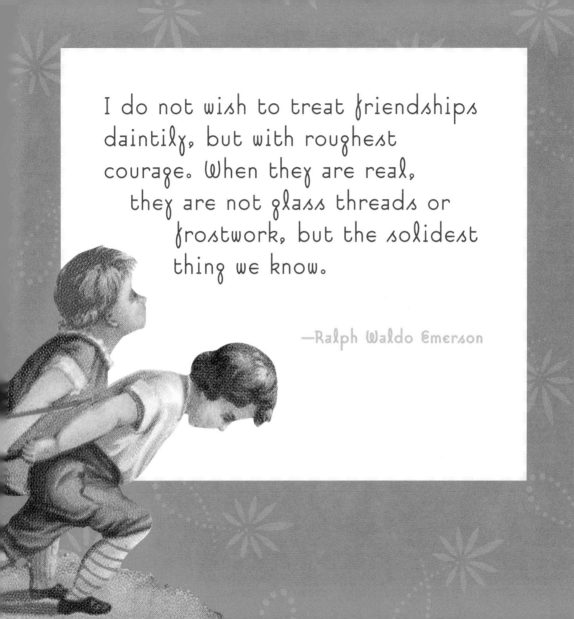

I do not wish to treat friendships daintily, but with roughest courage. When they are real, they are not glass threads or frostwork, but the solidest thing we know.

—Ralph Waldo Emerson

There are
friends, I think,
we can't imagine
living without.
People who are
sisters to us,
or brothers.

—Julie Reece Deaver

From *Othello*
by William Shakespeare

In act 3, scene 3, a misunderstanding (and Iago's treachery) has caused a rift in Othello's friendship with Cassio.

Desdemona: O, that's an honest fellow. Do not doubt, Cassio,

But I will have my lord and you again

As friendly as you were.

Cassio: Bounteous madam,

What ever shall become of Michael Cassio,

He's never anything but your true servant.

Desdemona: I know't; I thank you. You do love my lord;

You have known him long, and be you well assur'd

He shall in strangeness stand no farther off

Than in a politic distance.

Cassio: Ay, but, lady

That policy may either last so long,
Or feed upon such nice and waterish diet,
Or breed itself so out of circumstances,
That I being absent and my place supplied,
My general will forget my love and service.

Desdemona: Do not doubt that; before Emilia here,
I give thee warrant of thy place. Assure thee,
If I do vow a friendship, I'll perform it
To the last article. My lord shall never rest,
I'll watch him tame, and talk him out of patience,
His bed shall seem a school, his board a shrift,
I'll intermingle every thing he does
With Cassio's suit. Therefore be merry, Cassio,
For thy solicitor shall rather die
Than give thy cause away.

Silences make the real conversations between friends. Not the saying but the never needing to say is what counts.

—Margaret Lee Runbeck

May true friends be around you.

Of all that is near
Thou art the nearest
Of all that is dear
Thou art the dearest.

Companion

Centuries ago, the word *companion* described someone with whom you shared your bread. The word originated from the Old French word *compaignon*, and from the Vulgar Latin *compãniõ*, a compound noun formed from the Latin *com* (with) and *pãnis* (bread). The Old French stem *compaign-* also formed the basis of *compaignie*, which gave us the English word *company*.

THE ART OF LETTER WRITING

Nº XXII.
Place this Nº
After Page 2.

Write to me, tell me about your family, about the greatness, beauty
and sorrows of this life....

Believe me yours for ever,

Your friend,

—GEORGE SAND (PEN NAME OF AMANDINE-

AURORE-LUCILE, BARONNE DUDEVANT)

enturies ago, letters were written not just for the pleasure of sending and receiving them, but from sheer necessity. The telephone—not to mention the innumerable other forms of communication now available to us—had not yet been invented, and so friends and families conveyed both the good times and the bad via handwritten accounts.

News of Aunt Mary's recent nuptials or the sad and untimely passing of a childhood friend were received through "the post." One could be transported to exciting, faraway places by brother Robert's tales of his European travels, and rereading a love letter from an old (but not forgotten) beau could bring back fond, if not tearful, memories.

Letters can be written anywhere, any time of day—while you're waiting for the spin cycle on the washer to finish or sitting on the train during your daily commute to work. They can be quick, short notes just to say, "I'm thinking of you!" or they can be several pages filled with plans for a dream house or details about a mutual friend's river-rafting adventure.

Though few of us write letters with much frequency anymore, getting back in the habit is simple. Having a supply of beautiful stationery, fun cards, and photographs on hand can make the process more enjoyable—not only for you, but also for those who receive your letters. Elegant, monogrammed stationery (which also makes a lovely gift for a friend), wax and seals, and perfumed papers are just a few ways to further personalize your correspondence. So take a cue from the following "famous" letter writers and pick up pen and paper and begin (or start anew) your own fascinating journey in ink with a friend or two.

We have never talked together the way we have sometimes in letters. Why do I meet people better in letters?

—Anne Morrow Lindbergh

It's the ones
you can call up
at 4:00 A.M.
that matter.

—Marlene Dietrich

Peter Abelard and Héloïse

*P*eter Abelard (1079–c. 1144) was a French philosopher and theologian whose reputation as a teacher and original thinker made him one of the most well-known people of the twelfth century.

Héloïse (c. 1098–1164) was the niece of the canon of Notre-Dame, in Paris, and was tutored by Abelard. Later, she became the abbess of a convent founded by Abelard.

What cannot letters inspire? They have souls; they can speak; they have in them all that force which expresses the transports of the heart; they have all the fire of our passions, they can raise them as much as if the persons themselves were present; they have all the tenderness and the delicacy of speech, and sometimes even a boldness of expression beyond it.

—LETTER TO PETER ABELARD, FROM HÉLOÏSE

Agnes Porter

*A*gnes Porter (d. 1814) was a governess between the years of 1784 and 1806 to the children and grandchildren of an English aristocratic family. In addition to teaching children, Miss Porter spent much of her time attending balls and parties, and making trips to London and to the popular resort towns of Bath and Malvern.

My Dear Lady Mary,

Thank you for your nice little notes which always give me pleasure, but I think you are rather mistaken in your idea of letterwriting, so I shall in this leisure half-hour give you my opinion on that subject, and when we meet we will compare our sentiments together.

A letter to a friend seems to me simply this: giving them an hour of your company, notwithstanding whatever distance separates you. To do this is to convey your thoughts to them while you are writing. It little signifies what scenes surround you or what company you see—no, it is yourself your friend requires, and extraneous circumstances have no farther weight than as they affect and interest you. It is what you do; what you think; what you hope, fear, expect or wish, that forms matter for a friendly correspondence and, if you are in a state of perfect tranquillity, the calm transcripts of a serene mind must give delight to the eye of friendship. So write me as short letters as you please, but no more tell me that "the place affords no subjects." . . .

. . . embrace the dear children for me; and think sometimes, my dear Lady Mary, of your very sincere friend,

Agnes Porter

—LETTER TO LADY MARY FOX STRANGWAYS, MARCH 12, 1793, FROM AGNES PORTER

Gentle ladies, you will
remember till old age
what we did together in
our brilliant youth!

—Sappho

Are we not like two volumes of one book?

—Marceline Desbordes-Valmore

Charlotte Brontë

*C*harlotte Brontë (1816–1855), along with her two sisters, Emily and Anne, was an English novelist whose works are considered classics. Charlotte and Emily attended the Clergy Daughters' School in Cowan Bridge with their older sisters, Maria and Elizabeth. The school was the model for the infamous Lowood School of Charlotte's famous novel *Jane Eyre*.

LETTERS

Thank you for your letter; it was as pleasant as a quiet chat, as welcome as spring showers, as reviving as a friend's visit....

—LETTER TO A FRIEND, JULY 9, 1853,

FROM CHARLOTTE BRONTË

Jane Austen

*J*ane Austen (1775–1817), considered the creator of the English novel of manners, was educated at home along with her seven brothers and sisters. Austen began writing novels for her family when she was a child. Her best-known novels include *Sense and Sensibility* (1811), *Pride and Prejudice* (1813), *Mansfield Park* (1814), *Emma* (1815), and *Persuasion* (1817).

You are inimitable, irresistible. You are the delight of my life. Such letters, such entertaining letters, as you have lately sent!—such a description of your queer little heart!—such a lovely display of what imagination does. You are worth your weight in gold, or even in the new silver coinage. I cannot express to you what I have felt in reading your history of yourself, how full of pity and concern and admiration and amusement I have been. You are the paragon of all that is silly and sensible, common-place and eccentric, sad and lively, provoking and interesting....You are so odd!—and all the time, so perfectly natural—so peculiar in yourself, and yet so like everybody else!

It is very, very gratifying to me to know you so intimately. You can hardly think what a pleasure it is to me, to have such thorough pictures of your heart.

—LETTER TO FANNY KNIGHT, FROM JANE AUSTEN

. . . Friendships aren't perfect and yet they are very precious. For me, not expecting perfection all in one place was a great release.

—Letty Cottin Pogrebin

It seems to me that trying to live without friends is like milking a bear to get cream for your morning coffee. It is a whole lot of trouble, and then not worth much after you get it.

—Zora Neale Hurston

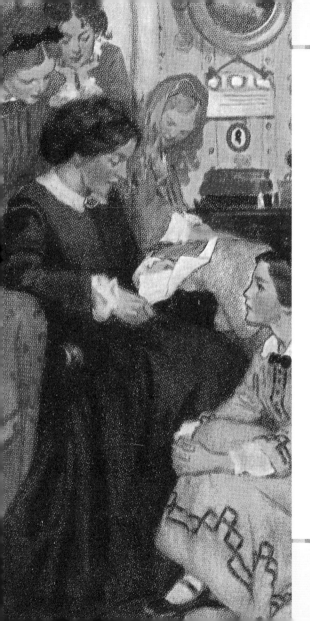

The big house did prove a Palace Beautiful, though it took some time for all to get in, and Beth found it very hard to pass the lions. **Old Mr. Laurence** was the biggest one; but after he had called, said something funny or kind to each one of the girls, and talked over old times with their mother, nobody felt much afraid of him, except timid Beth. The other lion was the fact that they were poor and Laurie rich; for this made them shy of accepting favours which they could not return. But, after a while, they found that he considered them the benefactors, and could not do enough to show how grateful he was for Mrs. March's motherly welcome, their cheerful society, and the comfort he took in that humble home of theirs. So they soon forgot their pride, and inter- changed kindnesses without stopping to think which was the greater.

All sorts of pleasant things happened about that time; for the new friendship flourished like grass in spring. Every one liked Laurie, and he privately informed his tutor that "the Marches were regularly splendid girls." With the delightful enthusiasm of youth, they took the solitary boy into their midst, and made much of him, and he found something very charming in the innocent companionship of these simple-hearted girls. Never having known mother or sisters, he was quick to feel the influences they brought about him; and their busy, lively ways made him ashamed of the indolent life he led. He was tired of books, and found people so interesting now, that Mr. Brooke was obliged to make very unsatisfactory reports; for Laurie was always playing truant, and running over to the Marches.

"Never mind; let him take a holiday, and make it up afterwards," said the old gentleman. "The good lady next door says he is studying too hard, and needs young society, amusement, and exercise. I suspect she is right, and that I've been coddling the fellow as if I'd been his grandmother. Let him do what he likes, as long as he is happy. He can't get into mischief in that little nunnery over there; and Mrs. March is doing more for him than we can."

What good times they had, to be sure! Such plays and tableaux, such sleigh-rides and skating frolics, such pleasant evenings in the old parlour, and now and then such gay little parties at the great house. Meg could walk in the conservatory whenever she liked, and revel in bouquets; Jo browsed over the new library voraciously, and con-vulsed the old gentleman with her criticisms; Amy copied pictures, and enjoyed beauty to her heart's content; and Laurie played "lord of the manor" in the most delightful style.

A Mile with Me

O who will walk a mile with me

Along life's merry way?

A comrade blithe and full of glee,

Who dares to laugh out loud and free,

And let his frolic fancy play,

Like a happy child, through the flowers gay

That fill the field and fringe the way

Where he walks a mile with me.

And who will walk a mile with me

Along life's weary way?

A friend whose heart has eyes to see

The stars shine out o'er the darkening lea,

And the quiet rest at the end o' the day,—

A friend who knows, and dares to say,

The brave, sweet words that cheer the way

Where he walks a mile with me.

With such a comrade, such a friend,

I fain would walk till journey's end,

Through summer sunshine, winter rain,

And then?—Farewell, we shall meet again!

——Henry van Dyke

More Fun Things for Friends

○ Build a dollhouse from scratch, then scour garage sales for miniature furniture to fill it.

○ Have a cookie bake-off (for the most sinful, simple, or exotic cookie)—then a taste-test. Have plenty of milk, lemonade, or iced tea on hand to refresh your palate.

○ Sign up for a kick-boxing, yoga, or other exercise class; help each other stick with it and make it more fun.

to Do Together

○ Indulge in a day of beauty (facial, manicure, or pedicure), either at a salon or in the comfort and privacy of your own home.

○ Reconnect with old (and new) friends by writing a letter in which you detail one of your favorite memories of the two of you together.

From *The Woman's Rose*

by Olive Schreiner

It is many years ago now; I was a girl of fifteen, and I went to visit in a small up-country town. It was young in those days, and two days' journey from the nearest village; the population consisted mainly of men. A few were married, and had their wives and children, but most were single. There was only one young girl there when I came. She was about seventeen, fair, and rather fully-fleshed; she had large dreamy blue eyes, and wavy light hair; full, rather heavy

lips, until she smiled; then her face broke into dimples, and all her white teeth shone. The hotel-keeper may have had a daughter, and the farmer in the outskirts had two, but we never saw them. She reigned alone. All the men worshipped her. . . .

Then I came. I do not think I was prettier; I do not think I was so pretty as she was. I was certainly not as handsome. But I was vital, and I was new, and she was old—they all forsook her and followed me. They worshipped me. . . .

Only one thing took from my pleasure; I could not bear that they had deserted her for me. I liked her great dreamy blue eyes, I liked her slow walk and drawl; when I saw her sitting among men, she seemed to me much too good to be among them; I would have given all their compliments if she would once have smiled at me as she smiled at them, with all her face breaking into radiance, with her dimples and flashing teeth. But I knew it never could be; I felt sure she hated me; that she wished I was dead; that she wished I had never come to the village. She did not know, when we went out riding, and a man who had always ridden beside her came to ride beside me, that I sent him away; that once when a man thought to win my favour by ridiculing her slow drawl before me I turned on him so fiercely that he never dared come before me again. I knew she knew that at the hotel men had made a bet as to which was the prettier, she or I, and had asked each man who came in, and that the one who had staked on me won. I hated them for it, but I would not let her see that I cared about what she felt towards me.

She and I never spoke to each other.

If we met in the village street we bowed and passed on; when we shook hands we did so silently, and did not look at each other. But I thought she felt my presence in a room just as I felt hers.

At last the time for my going came. I was to leave the next day. Some one I knew gave a party in my honour, to which all the village was invited.

It was midwinter; there was nothing in the gardens but a few dahlias and chrysanthemums, and I suppose that for two hundred miles round there was not a rose to be bought for love or money. Only in the garden of a friend of mine, in a sunny corner between the oven and the brick wall, there was a rose tree growing which had on it one bud. It was white, and it had been promised to the fair haired girl to wear at the party.

The evening came; when I arrived and went to the waiting-room, to take off my mantle, I found the girl there already. She was dressed in pure white, with her great white arms and shoulders showing, and her bright hair glittering in the candle-light, and the white rose fastened at her breast. She looked like a queen. I said "Good evening," and turned away quickly to the glass to arrange my old black scarf across my old black dress.

Then I felt a hand touch my hair.

"Stand still," she said.

I looked in the glass. She had taken the white rose from her breast, and was fastening it in my hair.

"How nice dark hair is; it sets off flowers so." She stepped back and looked at me. "It looks much better there!"

I turned round.

"You are so beautiful to me," I said.

"Y-e-s," she said, with her slow Colonial drawl; "I'm so glad."

We stood looking at each other.

Then they came in and swept us away to dance. All the evening we did not come near to each other. Only once, as she passed, she smiled at me.

The next morning I left the town.

I never saw her again.

Years afterwards I heard she had married and gone to America; it may or may not be so—but the rose—the rose is in the box still! When my faith in woman grows dim, and it seems that for want of love and magnanimity she can play no part in any future heaven; then the scent of that small withered thing comes back:—spring cannot fail us.

. . . I have learned that to have a good friend is the purest of all God's gifts, for it is a love that has no exchange of payment.

—Frances Farmer

Yes'm, old friends is always best,
'less you can catch a new one that's
fit to make an old one out of.

—Sarah Orne Jewett

A Portrait of Friendship

In the forbidding environment of Australia, old friends are reunited.

We drove to Meekatharra . . . to pick up Jen and Toly. . . . I couldn't speak when I first saw them, but I held on to them tight. Seeing them and touching them was like a dose of tonic. They understood. They stroked my ruffled feathers and forced me to laugh.

—Robyn Davidson, *Tracks*

George Eliot

The London home of English novelist Marian Evans (1819–1880), who published books under the pseudonym George Eliot, was at the center of Victorian intellectual literary life. Eliot's books include *Adam Bede* (1859), *Silas Marner* (1861), and *Middlemarch* (1871–1872).

Dearest Friend,

...I am sure nobody cares for nobody more than I care for you, and as for having one's dearest friends under the same meridian with one, that would be to have two **summa bona** at once, which is clearly contrary to the law or method of nature.

I shall write to you all in a day or two, so I tell you no news. This is only to assure you that your little notes are very precious to me, whether I answer them or not. I am sorely disappointed when I have none of your handwriting. In short you are the dearest, oldest, stupidest, tiresomest, delightfullest, and never-to-be-forgotten-est of friends to me and I am ever

Your affectionate

Marian

—LETTER TO CHARLES BRAY, JANUARY 17, 1853, FROM GEORGE ELIOT

Emily Dickinson

*E*mily Elizabeth Dickinson (1830–1886) was born in Amherst, Massachusetts, to a very religious family whose roots in New England spanned some eight generations. Dickinson was educated at Amherst Academy and Mount Holyoke Female Seminary in Massachusetts. She is widely considered a major American poet for her unique and perceptive approach to such universal subjects as love and death. Dickinson was a spirited, active woman who later withdrew from the public; her only contact with her friends, in her later life, was through her whimsical, witty letters.

And thank you for my dear letter, which came on Saturday night, when all the world was still; thank you for the love it bore me, and for its golden thoughts, and feelings so like gems, that I was sure I gathered them in whole baskets of pearls!

—LETTER TO A FRIEND, FROM EMILY DICKINSON

A Portrait of Friendship

A nineteenth-century widow describes the intense friendship forged between her husband and another soldier during the Civil War.

If they'd been bosom friends when they left Falls, why they were beyond blood brothers now. Slept side by side, and when cannon fire got nearer and so loud, they'd scoot over and hold on to one another, all mashed cheek to jowl like puppies in a box . . .

—Allan Gurganus, *Oldest Living Confederate Widow Tells All*

I often think,
how could I have
survived without
these women?

—Claudette Renner

From *Olive*
by Dinah Maria Mulock Craik

There is a deep beauty—more so than the world will acknowledge—in this impassioned first friendship, most resembling first love, whose faint shadowing it truly is. Who does not, even while smiling at its apparent folly, remember the sweetness of such a dream? Many a mother with her children at her knee, may now and then call to mind some old playmate, for whom, when they were girls together, she felt such an intense love. How they used to pine for the daily greeting—the long walk, fraught with all sorts of innocent secrets. Or, in absence, the almost interminable letters—positive love-letters, full of "dearest"s and "beloved"s, and sealing-wax kisses. Then the delicious meetings—sad partings, also quite lover-like in the multiplicity of tears and embraces—embraces sweeter than those of all the world beside—and tears, but our own are gathering while we write— Ah! . . .

Sara Derwent . . . completely charmed the simple Olive with her beauty, her sparkling, winning cheerfulness, and her ready sympathy. So they became the most devoted friends. Not a day passed without their spending some portion of it together—Olive teaching the young Londoner the pleasures of the country; and Sara, in her turn, inducting the wondering Olive into all the delightful mysteries of life, as learnt in a large home circle, and a still larger circle of society. Olive, not taking aught from the passionate love with which she looked up to her mother, yet opened her warm heart to the sweetness of this affection—so fresh, so sudden, so full of sympathetic contact. It was like a new revelation in her girlhood—the satisfying of a thirst, just beginning to be felt. She thought of Sara continually; delighted in being with her; in admiring her beauty, and making interests out of every interest of hers. And to think that her friend loved her in return, brought a sensation of deep happiness, not unmixed with gratitude.

Friends gotta trust each other . . . 'cause ain't nothin' like a true friend.

—Mildred D. Taylor

Susan B. Anthony and Elizabeth Cady Stanton

Friends since they first met each other in 1851, Susan B. Anthony and Elizabeth Cady Stanton fought for a woman's right to vote and to change laws in New York, to give women control over their property, wages, and children. Although neither Anthony nor Stanton lived to see women get the vote, their friendship—and collaboration—lasted for fifty-two years.

Androcles and the Lion
by Aesop

Androcles was a Roman slave who was treated cruelly by his master. Deciding to run away, Androcles slipped out from his room one night, and fled into the hostile desert that surrounded his master's home. Courageous and determined, Androcles knew that he'd be killed if he were captured. He also knew that he might face a terrible death in the desert. He might starve, or die of thirst, or even become a meal for a wild beast. Whatever the outcome, he decided, it was better than being a slave any longer.

After wandering the desert for two days, Androcles, weak with hunger and suffering from the intense heat, stumbled upon a dark cave. Inside there was water, but also . . . a lion!

Androcles could not escape, and so he awaited the lion's

attack. Instead, the huge lion moved slowly, moaning in pain: There was a thorn in his paw. Androcles forgot his fear and quickly helped the lion by remov-ing the thorn from his paw.

The lion gratefully licked Androcles' face, and a most unusual friendship was born. Free and protected by the lion,

Androcles was finally happy. The lion, glad for a friend, was also content. For three years, the man and beast lived together in the cave, until one day, Roman soldiers discovered Androcles, and taking him captive, returned him to Rome.

His former master ordered Androcles to be thrown to the lions in the public arena, known as the Circus Maximus. Many slaves were thrown into the arena, to be eaten alive by fero-cious animals kept in the arena's cages. The emperor, Tiberius, along with the citizens of Rome, watched the slaves' ordeal as a popular form of entertainment.

Androcles was sent out to the middle of the ring, where he waited to die. A hungry lion was soon turned loose upon him, and the crowds roared their approval. The lion charged toward Androcles, but stopped suddenly. As the for-mer slave looked up from the ground, he recognized his only friend, the lion! Reunited, the two grasped each other and the lion licked Androcles' face.

Stunned, the crowds fell silent. Tiberius then ordered Androcles to be brought before him and demanded an explanation. Why had the lion spared his life? Androcles told the emperor the story of his escape into the desert and how he and the lion had became the best of friends.

Tiberius then decreed that the people in the arena should decide Androcles' fate. The crowd began to chant, "Free them!" and so the lion and Androcles were set free. As they walked triumphantly through the streets of Rome, citizens showered them with coins and flowers, marveling at the friendship that saved a man's, and a lion's, life.

In meeting again after a separation, acquaintances ask after our outward life, friends after our inner life.

—Marie von Ebner-Eschenbach

I believe that we are always attracted to what we need most, an instinct leading us toward the persons who are to open new vistas in our lives and fill them with new knowledge.

—Helene Iswolski

4 March

Miss Sanxay drank tea with us—a very happy day in my brother and sister's company. She is one [of] the most charming women I know—amiable in her person, lively in discourse, of the sweetest temper and most benevolent disposition—in music an angel, and clever at every thing. We work, we chat, we walk and are happy together.

Letter to Her Sister, Cassandra

from Jane Austen

I have now attained the true art of letter-writing, which, we are always told, is to express on paper exactly what one would say to the same person by word of mouth; I have been talking to you almost as fast as I could the whole of this letter....

Sir, more than kisses,
letters mingle souls.
For, thus friends
absent speak.

—John Donne

Comrade

One's *comrade*, according to early French and Spanish translations, is someone with whom one shares a room. The word came from the French *camerade* and the Spanish *camarada*, or "room-sharer." Today's *camaraderie* is a nineteenth-century word borrowed from the French.

A Portrait of Friendship

While stitching together a quilt, Marianna and Constance—two women who normally keep to themselves—nevertheless form a friendship.

Marianna has lived such a private, interior life that, as much as she likes Constance, she still cannot reveal herself. It is not her way, and she senses that Constance is the only woman in the quilting circle who would understand that because Constance is like her in that respect.

—Whitney Otto, *How to Make an American Quilt*

FOOD, FRIENDS, AND FUN

Friendship.

It is around the table that friends understand best the warmth of being together.

—Italian saying

What's more fun than "dinner and a movie"? Dinner, *friends*, and a movie about food and friends, of course! *The Big Chill* was a blockbuster film about a group of friends who gathered for the funeral of a mutual friend. It had wonderful actors, great music, and fabulous "food" scenes. . . . The kitchen was (and continues to be) the place where everyone gathered to eat, dance, reminisce, and discover new things about each other.

Other films featuring great "food scenes" include *Animal House* (for the ultimate in "food fights"), *Babette's Feast* (about a French chef who cooks a spectacular meal for a group of elderly Danish folk), and *The Wedding*

Banquet (which features far more interesting fare than the usual prime rib or chicken).

Why not create your own food-filmfest with these delicious recipes? Whether you serve up a Mexican fiesta for forty, a potluck supper for ten, or just a simple but delicious dessert for two, the following recipes will feed you as well as your many friendships.

The pleasure in giving a dinner is mostly the pleasure of giving yourself. The effort you take is your way of showing your company that you care about them enough to give them a good time.

—Marguerite Kelly and Elia Parsons

Old-Fashioned Blueberry Muffins

Muffins are perfect for an impromptu breakfast or midmorning coffee klatch with friends to catch up on news around the neighborhood or to choose a color swatch for the walls in your new office. For variety, use different fruits or berries, or a combination of fruits such as half blueberries, half raspberries. For an extra nutritional boost, substitute whole wheat pastry flour for half the all-purpose flour and add two tablespoons of toasted wheat germ.

No-stick cooking spray or paper liners

2 eggs

$\frac{1}{2}$ cup milk

$\frac{1}{2}$ cup nonfat plain yogurt

3 Tbsp. vegetable oil

$\frac{1}{2}$ cup sugar

2 cups all-purpose flour

4 tsp. baking powder

$\frac{1}{8}$ tsp. baking soda

$\frac{1}{2}$ tsp. salt (optional)

$^1/_2$ tsp. cinnamon

$^1/_2$ tsp. nutmeg

1 $^1/_2$ cups fresh blueberries, cleaned, rinsed, and dried on paper towels (if using frozen berries, do not thaw).

Preheat oven to 400 degrees. Coat muffin tins with cooking spray or use paper liners.

In a large bowl, mix the eggs, milk, yogurt, oil, and sugar. Sift the dry ingredients together and stir into the egg mixture just to blend, without overbeating. Fold in the berries. Spoon the batter evenly among the muffin cups. (Optional: Sprinkle some sugar mixed with cinnamon on top.) Bake for 20 minutes (a little longer if frozen berries are used) or until the muffins rise and are golden brown. Cool muffins in the pan on a wire rack.

Baked Pears in Ginger Cream

For an impressive dessert and an inventive way to get your family and friends to eat their daily helping of fruit, try this simple recipe.

1 ¹/₂ cups sugar

1 ¹/₂ cups water

1-inch piece fresh ginger root, peeled and thinly sliced

4 large pears

1 ¹/₂ cups heavy cream

1 tsp. vanilla extract

1 tsp. ground ginger

¹/₄ tsp. cinnamon

¹/₄ tsp. nutmeg

1 Tbsp. finely chopped fresh ginger

1 Tbsp. ginger syrup

Put 1 cup of sugar in a large saucepan along with the water and the sliced ginger root. Boil over medium-high heat until sugar dissolves, then reduce to a simmer. Peel pears, cut in half lengthwise, and remove the cores. Place each pear half in the simmering mixture and poach until tender (approximately 10 minutes).

Preheat oven to 350 degrees. In a bowl, whisk the cream with the remaining $\frac{1}{2}$ cup sugar, vanilla, ground ginger, cinnamon, nutmeg, fresh ginger, and ginger syrup. Arrange the pears, face down, in a greased baking dish that's big enough to hold the pears in a single layer. Spoon the cream mixture over the pears, allowing it to drip between them.

Bake for 40 minutes. Baste the pears with the cream for the first 20 minutes, until they are tender when pierced with a knife. The cream should be thick and bubbly. Cool before serving. Serves 4.

When I'm old and gray I want to have a house by the sea. And paint. With a lot of wonderful chums, good music, and booze around. And a damn good kitchen to cook in.

—Ava Gardner

May many
Friends complete
your joy!

A Portrait of Friendship

At a time when food and money were scarce for four friends, the ritual of dining together was something to look forward to.

What fine food we treated ourselves to with our meager allowances! We didn't notice that the dumplings were stuffed mostly with stringy squash and that the oranges were spotted with wormy holes. We ate sparingly . . . we had luxuries few people could afford. We were the lucky ones.

—Amy Tan, *The Joy Luck Club*

Life itself is the proper binge.

—Julia Child

South-of-the-Border "Lasagna"

This easy-to-make "lasagna" is ideal fare for Super Bowl Sunday or any other event that brings out both the guys and gals. Add a couple bowls of chips and salsa, a green salad, and your favorite beverages for a complete, hearty meal that's sure to please everyone.

1 large onion, chopped

3 garlic cloves, minced

3 tsp. water

2 $\frac{1}{2}$ tsp. olive oil

1 medium green bell pepper, seeded and chopped

1 medium red bell pepper, seeded and chopped

1 cup picante sauce (mild, medium, or hot)

1 15-ounce can tomato sauce

1 $\frac{1}{2}$ tsp. ground cumin

1 tsp. black pepper

1 tsp. chili powder

2 15-ounce cans black beans, rinsed and drained

16 6-inch corn tortillas

1 cup ricotta cheese

2 cups shredded cheddar cheese

1 large tomato, chopped (for garnish)

$\frac{1}{2}$ cup sour cream (for garnish)

Preheat oven to 350 degrees. In a skillet, combine onion, garlic, water, and oil. Cook over medium heat (while stirring) until onion is soft. Add more water if liquid evaporates. Add green and red bell peppers, picante sauce, tomato sauce, cumin, pepper, and chili powder. Simmer uncovered for approximately 5 minutes. Add beans and remove from stove.

Spread half the mixture evenly in bottom of a 9 $\frac{1}{2}$-by-13-inch baking pan. Place 8 tortillas on top of the mixture in an overlapping layer. Spread the ricotta cheese evenly over tortillas and top with half the cheddar cheese. Top with remaining 8 tortillas, then remaining mixture. Cover with aluminum foil and bake 30–35 minutes. Remove foil and sprinkle remaining cheddar cheese over top and bake, uncovered, for 5 minutes or until cheese is melted. Garnish with tomato and sour cream (optional). Serves 8.

For My Friend P'ei Ti

We've not seen each other

For far too long a time.

Each day at the stream,

I remember us, together arm in arm

Arm in arm, as one, we were,

And memory revives

The pain of that farewell.

If today's memory is so,

How deep was this feeling—then?

—Wang Wei

A Portrait of Friendship

Although Constance has lost her husband, she is not looking to fill all the empty hours with lively company. Instead, she appreciates the quiet support of two friends.

"What I like about you, Marianna," says Constance, "is that you remind me of Howell. You let me be. . . . You and Dean are the reasons I am not completely lonely." She places her hand over her heart, without awareness, leaving smudges of dirt on her shirt.

—Whitney Otto, *How to Make an American Quilt*

A Friend in Need

A friend in need is a friend indeed. The Latin saying is
Amicus certus in re incerta cernitur, or a sure friend is
made known when (one is) in difficulty.

. . . my friends have made the story of my life. In a thousand ways they have turned my limitations into beautiful privileges, and enabled me to walk serene and happy in the shadow cast by my deprivation.

—Helen Keller

True happiness consists not in the multitude of friends, but in the worth and choice.

—Ben Jonson

James Boswell

*J*ames Boswell (1740–1795) was a Scottish lawyer and the biographer of the famous English writer, Samuel Johnson. He also befriended during his lifetime some of the greatest thinkers in history, among them Voltaire and Rousseau.

When I sit down to write to you, I never think of making any apology, either of haste or any other impediment whatever. I consider you as a friend, who will take me just as I am, good, or bad, or indifferent.

—LETTER TO SIR DAVID DALRYMPLE, FROM

JAMES BOSWELL

John Keats

*E*nglish poet John Keats (1795–1821) was born in London and educated, at the age of fifteen, to be apprenticed to a surgeon. Keats studied medicine in London hospitals and became a licensed apothecary but never practiced his craft, opting instead to become a poet. Some of his most beloved poems include "Ode on a Grecian Urn," "The Eve of St. Agnes," and "Ode to a Nightingale."

LETTERS

My dear Keats,

... the Friends who surrounded me, were sensible to what talent I had,—but no one reflected my enthusiasm with that burning ripeness of soul, my heart yearned for sympathy,—believe me from my Soul in you I have found one,—you add fire, when I am exhausted, & excite fury afresh—I offer my heart & intellect & experience...

God bless you let our hearts be buried in each other

B. R. Haydon

—LETTER TO JOHN KEATS, MARCH 1817,
FROM BENJAMIN ROBERT HAYDON

. . . we must love our friends for *their* sakes rather than for *our own;* we must look at their truth to *themselves, full* as much as their truth to *us.*

—Charlotte Brontë

"Friendship's Tie."

Love sincere

Some of the most rewarding and beautiful moments of a friendship happen in the unforeseen open spaces between planned activities. It is important that you allow these spaces to exist.

—Christine Leefeldt and Ernest Callenbach

Georgia O'Keeffe and Anita Pollitzer

American abstract painter Georgia O'Keeffe (1887–1986), who is best known for her large paintings of flowers and cow skulls, met women's rights activist and art teacher Anita Pollitzer at Columbia University Teachers College in 1914, where they both were art students. Their friendship, which included the exchange of hundreds of letters, lasted for decades. O'Keeffe once said of friendship, "My friends are so much a part of my life that I always wish they all knew one another."

There's no friend like someone who has known you since you were five.

—Anne Stevenson

. . . One is taught
by experience to
put a premium on
those few people
who can appreciate
you for what you
are . . .

—Gail Godwin

A Portrait of Friendship

Five-year-old Scout narrates the time when she and her older brother, Jem, meet Dill for the first time.

That was the summer Dill came to us.

Early one morning . . . Jem and I heard something next door in Miss Rachel Haverford's collard patch. We went to the wire fence to see if there was a puppy . . . instead we found someone sitting looking at us. Sitting down, he wasn't much higher than the collards. We stared at him until he spoke:

"Hey."

"Hey yourself," said Jem pleasantly.

"I'm Charles Baker Harris," he said. "I can read."

"So what?" I said.

"I just thought you'd like to know I can read. You got anything needs readin' I can do it. . . ."

—*Harper Lee,* ***To Kill a Mockingbird***

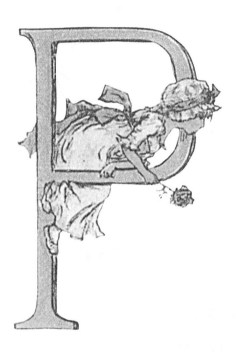

All food starting with p
is comfort food . . .
pasta, potato chips,
pretzels, peanut butter,
pastrami, pizza, pastry.

—Sara Paretsky

French Bread Pizza

When friends with children gather, dinner can sometimes resemble a three-ring circus. With this easy, tasty pizza recipe, the kids may actually stop bouncing on the furniture just long enough to create their own personal pizzas—and they may even eat them too! The beauty of this "recipe" is its versatility—you decide what the ingredients should be.

2 loaves French or Italian bread (each loaf equals 6 servings)

1 15-ounce can pasta sauce

1 red or green bell pepper, diced ($1/2$-inch pieces)

1 can green or black olives, sliced thin

1 stick pepperoni, sliced thin

1 12-ounce can artichoke hearts, washed and chopped

Sun-dried tomatoes

1 lb. mozzarella cheese, cubed or shredded

Seasonings to taste (pepper, oregano, basil, onion, and garlic powder)

Preheat oven to 350 degrees. (The above ingredients are all optional; use these suggestions or place your favorite pizza toppings in small bowls that will allow everyone to pick and choose what they like best.) Place bread slices, crust-side down, on baking sheets. With a large spoon, spread pasta sauce over the top of each slice. Then layer pepper, olives, pepperoni, artichoke hearts, and sun-dried tomatoes—or whatever you choose (ham and pineapple also work)—evenly over sauce. Last, sprinkle with cheese and seasonings.

Place cookie sheets with French bread pizzas in hot oven. Bake for approximately 20 minutes or until cheese has melted. Serve with a green salad or cup of soup.

If you accept a dinner invitation,
you have a moral obligation to be
amusing.

—Wallis Simpson, Duchess of Windsor

Summery Spinach Salad

Morning coffee with friends has carried over to the lunch hour? No problem! Show off your ability to "make do in a pinch" with this quick, healthy spinach salad. But be forewarned, when friends realize impromptu meals neither frazzle nor faze you, they may want to stay for dinner. . . .

2 lbs. raw spinach, washed, dried, stems removed

1 cup ricotta cheese

1 cup sliced raw mushrooms

2 hard-boiled eggs, sliced

1 cup pineapple chunks

²/₃ cup walnut pieces

6 strips bacon

5 Tbsp. olive oil

2 Tbsp. tarragon vinegar

1 tsp. mustard

Salt and pepper to taste

Tear the spinach into small pieces and mix with the ricotta cheese, mushrooms, egg slices, and pineapple chunks. Broil the walnuts and bacon until they are crisp. Crumble the bacon and add it, along with the nuts, to the spinach mixture. To make the dressing, combine oil, vinegar, mustard, salt, and pepper and pour over salad just before serving.

THE SWEETNESS
OF FRIENDS

Is there anything that makes life sweeter than possessing the loyalty and love of a few close friends, those people who know your foibles and quirks, have been with you through thick and thin, and will see you through the good times and the bad? *S*weet recipes are combined with sweet sentiments in this chapter, in honor of that sinfully delicious relationship we call *friendship!*

Orange Sugar Cookies

It's that time of year again, when someone needs cookies baked for school or charity or . . . dare we say . . . a sugar fit? Get your friends together for a cookie bake-off and share the wealth (everyone trade a dozen). This recipe for orange sugar cookies is sure to be a favorite: They're a snap to prepare and are practically guaranteed to bring back fond childhood memories. Don't forget to have plenty of milk on hand.

2 $\frac{1}{2}$ cups sifted all-purpose flour

2 tsp. baking powder

1 tsp. salt

$\frac{3}{4}$ cup butter

1 $\frac{1}{4}$ cups sugar

2 eggs

1 Tbsp. grated orange rind

2 Tbsp. orange-flavored liqueur (optional)

Preheat oven to 400 degrees. Sift together flour, baking powder, and salt. Beat together butter and 1 cup of the sugar in a large bowl, until blended; mix in eggs, orange rind, and liqueur. Add the flour mixture, one-third at a time, until well blended. Chill dough until firm (about one hour). Then, on a lightly floured surface, roll out dough to a ¼-inch thickness and sprinkle with the remaining sugar. Cut into rounds with a floured, 3-inch round cookie cutter (or use a drinking glass, turned upside down).

Place cookies on a large cookie sheet approximately 1 inch apart. Bake for 8–10 minutes or until firm. Remove and cool on wire rack.

Gingerbread Friends

Here's a new twist on an old favorite! The recipe is a classic—but you can make it your own by decorating the cookies to look like your best buddies!

1 Tbsp. water

1 egg

2 Tbsp. dark molasses

3 $\frac{1}{4}$ cups all-purpose flour

1 tsp. baking soda

$\frac{1}{2}$ tsp. salt

1 $\frac{1}{2}$ cups brown sugar

2 Tbsp. grated orange zest

1 $\frac{1}{2}$ tsp. cinnamon

1 tsp. ginger

$\frac{1}{2}$ tsp. nutmeg

$\frac{1}{8}$ tsp. cloves

1 cup unsalted butter, chilled, cut into 1-inch pieces

Preheat oven to 350 degrees. Stir the water, egg, and molasses together in a small bowl and set aside. In a food processor add flour, baking soda, salt, brown sugar, orange zest, and spices; blend for about 15 seconds. Add the butter and blend for another 30 seconds. Add the molasses mixture to the flour mixture and blend until the dough sticks together. Remove the dough from the blender and knead it for about 10–15 seconds.

Divide the dough into two pieces, wrap each one in plastic wrap, and refrigerate for about 90 minutes. Line two or three baking sheets with wax paper. Take one slab of chilled dough and place it between two new pieces of wax paper. Roll it out until it's about $\frac{1}{8}$ inch thick, then discard the top piece of wrap.

Cut out Gingerbread Friends using a 4- or 6-inch cookie cutter. With a spatula, place the cookies on the baking sheet. Leave about 1 inch between each cookie. Decorate the "friends" with a combination of currants, sprinkles, candies, and icing.

Repeat the above steps with the second slab of dough. Bake cookies for 12–15 minutes or until firm. Cool on wire racks.

Though Love be deeper, Friendship
is more wide.

—Corinne Roosevelt Robinson

Each friend represents a world in us, a world possibly not born until they arrive, and it is only by this meeting that a new world is born.

—Anaïs Nin

Untitled

She is like

a mother to me.

She embraces me

as if I were her child.

I want to follow

her footprints, for

she will not cast me off.

—Makeda, Queen of Sheba

A Night with My Friend

Spilling out a thousand cares,

Lifting a hundred cups of wine,

A good night, needing true conversation,

A blinding moon keeps us awake—

We lie down, surrounded by barren hills,

The sky and the grass are our sheets and pillow.

—Li Po

From *The Adventures of Huckleberry Finn*

by Mark Twain

So I started for town in the wagon, and when I was halfway I see a wagon coming, and sure enough it was Tom Sawyer, and I stopped and waited till he come along. I says "Hold on!" and it stopped alongside, and his mouth opened up like a trunk, and stayed so; and he swallowed two or three times like a person that's got a dry throat, and then says:

"I hain't ever done you no harm. You know that. So, then, what you want to come back and ha'nt *me* for?"

I says:

"I hain't come back—I hain't been *gone*."

When he heard my voice it righted him up some, but he warn't quite satisfied yet. He says:

"Don't you play nothing on

me, because I wouldn't on you. Honest injun, you ain't a ghost?"

"Honest injun, I ain't," I says.

"Well—I—I—well, that ought to settle it, of course; but I can't somehow seem to understand it no way. Looky here, warn't you ever murdered *at all?*"

"No. I warn't ever murdered at all—I played it on them. You come in here and feel of me if you don't believe me."

So he done it; and it satisfied him; and he was that glad to see me again he didn't know what to do.

Sydney Smith

Sydney Smith (1771–1845) was an English clergyman and essayist who was known for his great wit. He befriended Lady Georgiana, the wife of an English viscount, whom he met when he was a rector in Yorkshire. When she was pregnant and in low spirits, Smith wrote the following letter, in which he enumerated twenty ways by which she could cheer herself up.

Dear Lady Georgiana,

...Nobody has suffered more from low spirits than I have done—so I feel for you. 1st. Live as well as you dare. 2nd. Go into the shower-bath with a small quantity of water at a temperature low enough to give you a slight sensation of cold, 75° or 80°. 3rd. Amusing books. 4th. Short views of human life—not further than dinner or tea. 5th. Be as busy as you can. 6th. See as much as you can of those friends who respect and like you. 7th. And of those acquaintances who amuse you. 8th. Make no secret of low spirits to your friends, but talk of them freely....20th.
Believe me, dear Lady Georgiana,

Very truly yours,

Sydney Smith

—LETTER TO LADY GEORGIANA,

FEBRUARY 16, 1820, FROM SYDNEY SMITH

Letter to Charles Bray, July 27, 1849

from George Eliot

Dear Friend,

...I have made another friend, too—an elderly English lady [Mrs. Lock], who used to live at Ryde, and who has been staying here about a month—a pretty old lady with plenty of shrewdness and knowledge of the world. She began to say very kind things to me in rather a waspish tone yesterday morning at breakfast. I liked her better at dinner and tea, and today we are quite confidential. She has her little granddaughter with its nurse under her charge while the mamma is travelling. I only hope she will stay— she is just the sort of person I shall like to have to speak to—not at all "congenial" but with a character of her own....

Your affectionate

Pollian

A Portrait of Friendship

Anna Howard Shaw describes an unusual friendship she shared with a woman who lived next door to her family when Anna was a girl.

My second friendship, and one which had a strong influence on my after-life, was formed in Lawrence. I was not more than ten years old when I met this new friend, but the memory of her in after-years, and the impression she had made on my susceptible young mind, led me first into the ministry, next into medicine, and finally into suffrage-work. Living next door to us, on Prospect Hill, was a beautiful and mysterious woman. All we children knew of her was that

she was a vivid and romantic figure, who seemed to
have no friends and of whom our elders spoke in
whispers or not at all. To me she was a princess in a
fairy-tale. . . .

Very soon she noticed me. Possibly she saw the
adoration in my childish eyes. She began to nod
and smile at me, and then to speak to me . . . and
a strange friendship began and developed between
the woman of the town and the little girl she loved.
Some of those visits I remember as vividly as if I
had made them yesterday. There was never the
slightest suggestion during any of them of things I
should not see or hear, for while I was with her
my hostess became a child again, and we played

together like children. She had wonderful toys for me, and pictures and books; but the thing I loved best of all and played with for hours was a little stuffed hen which she told me had been her dearest treasure when she was a child at home. She had also a stuffed puppy, and she once mentioned that those two things alone were left of her life as a little girl. Besides the toys and books and pictures, she gave me ice-cream and cake, and told me fairy-tales. She had a wonderful understanding of what a child likes.

—Anna Howard Shaw, *The Story of a Pioneer*

Annie Cooper

*A*nnie Cooper was the youngest daughter in a large, wealthy family of boat builders from Sag Harbor, New York. From her diary entries (which she began in 1880, at the age of fifteen), it seems she led a happy, carefree childhood and later, as a young adult, studied art—drawing and painting—as did many young women of her time.

February 24

Oh! what a pleasure it is to have these two old friends look after us, & take us around! Oh, how thankful I am for it, Oh, my God, may it continue always, *this Platonic & true friendship, & grow more & more true & confiding & charming, & strong* forever & ever. *until we four meet in the Celestial Court above.*

—ANNIE COOPER, JOURNAL ENTRY

From the Journal of Agnes Porter

19 August

My dear friend Mrs. Simpson, Miss Hoare that was, came to see me. We had not met for sixteen years. She brought with her a fine boy, her only child, about twelve years old. She has lost her worthy husband. Our pleasure was mutual, and we reverted to the days that are passed and brought many a person and scene to recollection.

Silences make the real conversations between friends. Not the saying but the never needing to say is what counts.

—Margaret Lee Runbeck

I suppose there is one friend in the life of each of us who seems not a separate person, however dear and beloved, but an expansion, an interpretation, of one's self, the very meaning of one's soul.

—Edith Wharton

One Sister have I in the house—

One Sister have I in the house—
And one a hedge away.
There's only one recorded—
But both belong to me.

One came the road that I came—
And wore my last year's gown—
The other, as a bird her nest
Builded our hearts among.

She did not sing as we did—

It was a different tune—

Herself to her a music

As Bumble bee of June.

Today is far from childhood,

But up and down the hills,

I held her hand the tighter—

Which shortened all the miles—

And still her hum

The years among,

Deceives the Butterfly;

And in her Eye

The Violets lie,

Mouldered this many May—

I split the dew,

But took the morn—

I chose this single star

From out the wide night's numbers—

Sue—forevermore!

—Emily Dickinson

A Portrait of Friendship

Jem questions his new friend Dill about his age and his lengthy name.

". . . You look right puny for goin' on seven."

"I'm little but I'm old," he said.

Jem brushed his hair back to get a better look. "Why don't you come over, Charles Baker Harris?" he said. "Lord, what a name."

" 's not any funnier'n yours. Aunt Rachel says your name's Jeremy Atticus Finch."

Jem scowled. "I'm big enough to fit mine," he

said. "Your name's longer'n you are. Bet it's a foot longer."

"Folks call me Dill . . ."

—Harper Lee, *To Kill a Mockingbird*

Your sincere
Friend.

Untitled

This world is,

compared to You!

a body of water too tiny

to hold even a mustard seed.

—Lal Ded

When friends ask for a second cup
they are open to conversation. . . .

—Gail Parent

Mocha Float

After dinner with the gang, skip the usual pot of Joe and try this coffee-inspired dessert instead. It's sure to garner kudos for the host or hostess and requests for a second cup.

Freshly brewed hot coffee (for 4)
4 tsp. sugar (1 per glass)
4 tsp. vanilla extract (1 per glass)
Ice
Cream
1 scoop mocha or chocolate ice cream (per glass)

In a tall glass, dissolve sugar in the coffee. Add vanilla extract and stir. Top off each coffee cup with ice and cream and stir again. Add ice cream.

. . . we've been long together,
Through pleasant and through
cloudy weather.

—Anna Laetitia Barbauld

We are each
other's reference
point at our
turning points.

—Elizabeth Fishel

The Trees and the Axe
by Aesop

A woodsman came into a forest to ask the trees to give him a handle for his axe. It seemed such a modest request that the principal trees at once agreed to it, and it was decided that the plain homely ash should supply what was wanted. No sooner had the woodsman got what he needed, than he began laying about him on all sides with his axe, felling the noblest trees in the forest. The oak, now seeing the whole matter too late, whispered to the cedar, "We should never have given in to the first request; if we had not sacrificed our humble neighbor, we might have yet stood for ages ourselves."

Moral:

The betrayal of our
friends may result in
our own downfall.

The only good teachers for you are those friends who love you, who think you are interesting or very important, or wonderfully funny.

—Brenda Ueland

Your life and mine are just two threads in this eternal canvas. They diverge, converge, and interweave with each other, then diverge and converge again until the fabric is complete.

—Kahlil Gibran

. . . let us enjoy each other and
  be sure
that no rainburst or seas or
  seastorm lure
us to separation before our
  lives end . . .

—Louise Labé

A Portrait of Friendship

The family dog tells the story of a friendship that developed between himself and a human visitor during time spent together after meals.

A friend of the family who descends on us from time to time is one of the few people I know who shares my habit of relaxing under the dining table. . . . Once he has eaten, he has been known to slide gently down to join me, and we bond.

—Peter Mayle, *A Dog's Life*

A Sister

For there is no friend like a sister

In calm or stormy weather;

To cheer one on the tedious way,

To fetch one if one goes astray,

To lift one if one totters down,

To strengthen whilst one stands.

—Christina Georgina Rossetti

From "The Shelter"
by Jalal ad-Din ar-Rumi

Friend, our intimacy is like this:

Wherever you place your foot, I am there,

in the firmness beneath you.

I my Companions see
In You, another Me.

—Thomas Traherne

In real friendship the judgment, the genius, the prudence of each party become the common property of both.

—Maria Edgeworth

Even More Fun Things for Friends

- Create your own yearly tradition: high tea at a fancy hotel, running a local marathon to support a good cause, a weekend camping trip, or a filmfest of your favorite flicks.

- Plan a monthly adventure with a group of friends. Each person takes turns planning the event—hot-air ballooning, horseback riding, gallery hopping, hiking. Set a price and time limit, but let your imagination run wild!

to Do Together

∘ Designate—and decorate—one room or small portion of your home with pictures of your friends. Create a frame that matches each friend's unique personality.

∘ Host a thematic potluck dinner once a month: "Grandma's favorite recipe" night, "international cuisine" lunch, or "just desserts."

∘ Start your own book club (or join an already existing one)— choose a mutually agreed-upon book to read, then meet again to discuss its merits and how it affected you.

What a luxury it was
to spend time with
old friends with whom
it was okay to talk
about nothing much.

—Lisa Alther

There are people whom one loves immediately and for ever. Even to know they are alive in the world with one is quite enough.

—Nancy Spain

Letter to Sara Hennell,
October 31, 1854
from George Eliot

My dear Sara

... I love Cara and you with unchanged and unchangeable affection, and while I retain your friendship I retain the best that life has given me next to that which is the deepest and gravest joy in all human experience.

Marian Evans

In fond remembrance

To my friend I write a letter and from him I receive a letter. That seems to you a little. It suffices me. It is a spiritual gift, worthy of him to give and of me to receive.

—Ralph Waldo Emerson

My own dear Abiah,

For so I will still call you, though while I do it, even now I tremble at my strange audacity, and almost wish I had been a little more humble not quite so presuming.

Six long months have tried hard to make us strangers, but I love you better than ever notwithstanding the link which bound us in that golden chain is sadly dimmed, I feel more reluctant to lose you from that bright circle, whom I've called my friends. I mailed a long letter to you the 1st of March, & patiently have I waited a reply, but none has yet cheered me.

Slowly, very slowly, I came to the conclusion that you had forgotten me, & I tried to forget you, but your image still haunts me, and tantalizes me with fond recollections. At our Holyoke Anniversary, I caught one glimpse of your face, & fondly anticipated an interview with you, & a reason for your silence, but when I thought to find you search was vain, for "the bird had flown." Sometimes, I think it was a fancy, think I did not really see my old friend, but her spirit, then your well known voice tells me it was no spirit, but yourself, living, that stood within that crowded hall & spoke to me—Why did you not come back that day, and tell me what had sealed your lips toward me? Did my letter never reach you, or did you coolly decide to love me, & write to me no more? If you love me, & never received my letter—then may you think yourself wronged, and that rightly, but if you don't want to be my friend any longer, say so, & I'll try once more to blot you from my memory. Tell me very soon, for suspense is intolerable. I need not tell you, this is from,

Emilie

A friend doesn't go on a diet because you are fat. A friend never defends a husband who gets his wife an electric skillet for her birthday. A friend will tell you she saw your old boyfriend—and he's a priest.

—Erma Bombeck

Though our communication
wanes at times of
absence, I'm aware of a
strength that emanates in
the background.

—Claudette Renner

A Portrait of Friendship

An Australian adventure tests the bonds of friendship between the author, Robyn, and her new friend, Rick.

. . . . the friendship was firmly cemented. It had a rock-hard basis called shared experience, or the tolerance developed from seeing someone at their best and at their worst, and stripped of all social value—the bare bones of another human being.

—Robyn Davidson, *Tracks*

Friendship

Oh, the comfort—the inexpressible comfort
  of feeling safe with a person,
Having neither to weigh thoughts,
Nor measure words—but pouring them
All right out—just as they are—
Chaff and grain together—

Certain that a faithful hand will

Take and sift them—

Keep what is worth keeping—

And with the breath of kindness

Blow the rest away.

—Dinah Maria Mulock Craik

We Have Been Friends Together

We have been friends together,

In sunshine and in shade;

Since first beneath the chestnut trees

In infancy we played.

But coldness dwells within thy heart—

A cloud is on thy brow;

We have been friends together—

Shall a light word part us now?

We have been gay together;

We have laughed at little jests;

For the fount of hope was gushing,

Warm and joyous, in our breasts.

But laughter now hath fled thy lip,

And sullen glooms thy brow;

We have been gay together—

Shall a light word part us now?

We have been sad together—

We have wept, with bitter tears,

O'er the grass-grown graves, where slumbered

The hopes of early years.

The voices which are silent there

Would bid thee clear thy brow;

We have been sad together—

O! what shall part us now?

—Caroline Norton

So long as we love we serve; so long as we are loved by others, I would almost say that we are indispensable.

—Robert Louis Stevenson

A Portrait of Friendship

Corrina and Hy's friendship has developed through the rituals, both modest and grand, of daily life.

Corrina Amurri and Hy Dodd go back many years. Their boys, Laury and Will, were born only a few months apart. The women gave each other baby showers, had coffee together . . . alternated lunch times at each other's homes, traded baby-sitting services. Quilted together at Glady Joe's.

—Whitney Otto, *How to Make an American Quilt*

Almost every
person has
something
secret he
likes to eat.

—M. F. K. Fisher

Caribbean Delight

You won't be able to keep this recipe a secret for long, which is fine as long as your friends remember to invite you over when it's their turn to dish it out. This fruity concoction is the perfect ending to a backyard barbecue with friends and family or as a sinful snack when your pals have gathered for an evening of trivia games or video viewing.

1 fresh pineapple, cut lengthwise; do not remove leaves or stem
2 medium mangos, cut into 1-inch pieces
2 mandarin oranges, sectioned
2 bananas, sliced
Juice of 1 lemon
1 cup fresh strawberries, sliced
1 cup guava, sliced
5 Tbsp. sugar
4 Tbsp. curaçao
3 cups vanilla ice cream
5 Tbsp. grated coconut

Hollow out the pineapple halves and cut its fruit into cubes; refrigerate the two halves. Combine pineapple cubes with the mangos, mandarin oranges, bananas (to keep bananas fresh looking, pour lemon juice over them), strawberries, and guava in a large bowl. Add sugar and curaçao. Scoop vanilla ice cream into the pineapple shell and top with the fruit. Sprinkle dish with grated coconut, then chill until ready to serve.

A Portrait of Friendship

The friendship between Dill and Jem is cemented after young Scout badgers Dill about his absent father.

I asked Dill where his father was: "You ain't said anything about him."

"I haven't got one."

"Is he dead?"

"No . . ."

"Then if he's not dead you've got one, haven't you?"

Dill blushed and Jem told me to hush, a sure sign that Dill had been studied and found acceptable.

—Harper Lee, *To Kill a Mockingbird*

I always felt that the great high privilege, relief and comfort of friendship was that one had to explain nothing.

—Katherine Mansfield

The balm of
life, a kind and
faithful friend.

—Mercy Otis Warren

13 September

A letter from my dear Miss Mitchell informed me of her marriage to Mr. Alexander of the twelfth of last month. I rejoiced to hear that so amiable and worthy a woman is now settled for life, and has a friend and protector—yet it breaks into my future prospect of spending my evening of life with her. No matter—it is for her advantage she should not, and that friendship deserves not the name which loses not its own partial views in the larger prospect of another's happiness.

Letter to Sara Hennell,
November 20, 1868
from George Eliot

My dear Sara…

…Our friend Mr. Spencer is growing younger with the years. He really looks brighter and more enjoying than he ever did before since he was in the really young, happy time of fresh discussion and inquiry. He always asks with sympathetic interest (proportion gardée, for you know his feelings are never too much for him) how you are going on. Unhappily I can never tell him much about you. His is a friendship which wears well, because of his truthfulness: that makes amends for many deficits. He is just come to ask George to walk out with him, and I wind up my hasty letter, that it may be carried to the post. All blessings to you dear Sara!

Your ever loving

Pollian

Trouble is a sieve
through which we sift
our acquaintances.
Those too big to pass
through are our friends.

—Arlene Francis

. . . the responsibilities of friendship? . . . To talk. And to listen.

—Rosie Thomas

Coffee Ecstasy

Do your friends often wonder how you manage to keep your cool when every-one around you is stressed out? Perhaps one of your secrets is this delightful "dessert" recipe. Be a real friend and share it (along with some of your other secrets!).

3 egg whites
1/4 cup sugar
Freshly brewed coffee
1 pint chocolate, vanilla, or coffee ice cream
1/4 cup toasted almonds, chopped (optional)
Cinnamon

Separate egg whites from yolks and discard yolks. In a small bowl, beat the egg whites, adding sugar slowly, until soft peaks form. Pour coffee evenly into 4 glasses. Spoon the egg whites on top, and add ice cream. Sprinkle drinks with toasted almonds and cinnamon.

All Paths Lead to You

All paths lead to you
Where e'er I stray,
You are the evening star
At the end of day.

All paths lead to you
Hill-top or low,
You are the white birch
In the sun's glow.

All paths lead to you

Where e'er I roam.

You are the lark-song

Calling me home!

—Blanche Shoemaker Wagstaff

Friends Taking Their Leave

Emerald hills slope down from the northern wall,

Rapid water rounds the eastern city.

Once separated from here,

The lone weed will tumble thousands of miles.

Clouds drift—a traveler's thoughts.

Sun sets—dear friend's heart.

Wave hands—we take our leave now,

Our reluctant horses neigh good-bye.

—*Li Po*

Another I.

—Zeno

Here's to you, old friend, may you
   live a thousand years,
Just to sort of cheer things in this
   vale of human tears;
And may I live a thousand too—a
   thousand—less a day,
'Cause I wouldn't care to be on
   earth and hear you'd passed away.

—Anonymous toast

"Auld Lang Syne"
by Robert Burns

Should auld acquaintance be forgot,

And never brought to mind?

Should auld acquaintance be forgot,

And days of Auld Lang Syne?

For Auld Lang Syne, my dear,

For Auld Lang Syne,

We'll tak' a cup o' kindness yet

For Auld Lang Syne!

We twa hae rin about the braes,

And pu'd the gowans fine;

But we've wandered monie a weary fit

Sin' Auld Lang Syne.

We twa hae paidl't i' the burn,

Frae mornin' sun till dine;

But seas between us braid hae roared

Sin' Auld Lang Syne.

And here's a hand, my trusty fiere,

And gie's a hand o' thine;

And we'll tak a right guid willie-waught

For Auld Lang Syne.

And surely ye'll be your pint-stowp,

And surely I'll be mine,

And we'll take a cup o' kindness yet

For Auld Lang Syne!

My letter as a bee, goes laden. Please love us and remember us. Please write us very soon, and tell us how you are . . .

—LETTER TO A FRIEND, FROM

EMILY DICKINSON

Book design and composition by Diane Hobbing
at Snap-Haus Graphics in Dumont, NJ

For Cynthia, Janis, and Cathy

—DSH